LAUGH

KU-533-638

ANDY CAPP

No. 11

PAWNBROKER

NOW THERE'S A SIGN OF A HARD WINTER—

PAW

Smythe

DRAWINGS BY REG SMYTHE

Prices: United Kingdom 15p. Australia 50 cents.
South Africa 45 cents.   New Zealand 45 cents.
Canada 75 cents.

© 1974 IPC Newspapers Ltd

Published by Daily Mirror Books,
79 Camden Road, Camden, London, NW1 9NT,
England

Printed in Great Britain by
Index Printers, Dunstable, Bedfordshire

ISBN 0 85939 019 5

A DAILY MIRROR RE-CAPP

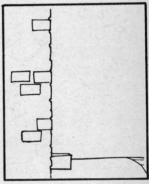

3

4

Smythe

1

2

3

YER'VE GOT T' KEEP ONE JUMP AHEAD

4

1

2

1

2

1

AFTER ALL THESE YEARS YER STILL LOOK AT ME TWICE, EH, PET?

YEH, PET

2

3

1

2

3

4

1

2

3

4

3

4

1

2

3

4

1

2

3

4

1

2

1

2

3

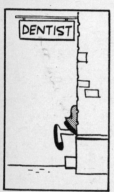

BY THE WAY, CHALKIE — WE'LL BE NEEDIN' SOME NEW CRICKET STUMPS BEFORE THE SEASON STARTS. REMIND ME TO BRING IT UP AT THE COMMITTEE MEETIN'.

I SHOULD 'AVE KEPT THE BOUQUET AN' THROWN THE *GROOM* AWAY!

1

2

3

4

1

2

3

4

A PENNY 'ERE, A PENNY THERE –!

1

2

2

3

4

1

2